Samuel French Acting Edition

Anti-Social

by Don Zolidis

SAMUELFRENCH.COM   SAMUELFRENCH.CO.UK

FOR PRODUCTION ENQUIRIES

UNITED STATES AND CANADA
Info@SamuelFrench.com
1-866-598-8449

UNITED KINGDOM AND EUROPE
Plays@SamuelFrench.co.uk
020-7255-4302

Each title is subject to availability from Samuel French, depending upon country of performance. Please be aware that *ANTI-SOCIAL* may not be licensed by Samuel French in your territory. Professional and amateur producers should contact the nearest Samuel French office or licensing partner to verify availability.

MUSIC USE NOTE

Licensees are solely responsible for obtaining formal written permission from copyright owners to use copyrighted music in the performance of this play and are strongly cautioned to do so. If no such permission is obtained by the licensee, then the licensee must use only original music that the licensee owns and controls. Licensees are solely responsible and liable for all music clearances and shall indemnify the copyright owners of the play(s) and their licensing agent, Samuel French, against any costs, expenses, losses and liabilities arising from the use of music by licensees. Please contact the appropriate music licensing authority in your territory for the rights to any incidental music.

IMPORTANT BILLING AND CREDIT REQUIREMENTS

If you have obtained performance rights to this title, please refer to your licensing agreement for important billing and credit requirements.

ANTI-SOCIAL was first performed at YES Preparatory School on April 15, 2018. The production was directed by Anthony Lane, and the original cast was as follows:

PARENTAL OVERSIGHT

MOM...Mara Marian
DAD ....Hector Estrada
ALLIA .... Heidi Alanis
MAGDA.. Jennifer Lopez

THE PRICE OF YOUTUBE FAME

TONI... Mario Medrano
DRAKE .... Carlos Mendez
JAMISON .... David Zamarripa
MOM... David Zamarripa

TROLLZ

MAGGIE..Nathalie Sanchez
KERRY .... Brisa Medrano
BOBO..Reyna Torres
MONDO..Samantha Adams

VIRAL/RIVAL

AUSTIN.. Leon Godinez
BRENT..Jesus Jimenez
AMELIA.. Jaelys Gonzalez
BOSS..Daira Gonzalez

PINTEREST IS TOTALLY NOT MAKING YOU ASHAMED OF YOUR LIFE

HUNTER....................................... Roberto Jimenez
KYLIE ....Sonique Villagomez
MCQUAID .... Angelica DeLeon
ROBINSON ....Stephanie Lopez

FOLLOWERS

ASHLEY .... Wendy Castillo
BAILEY .... Diana Galvan

THE LAST LIVING MYSPACE USER

TOM ....Marco Tello
KATHY .... Kimberly Jimenez
JANITOR.. Sarai Hernandez

CHARACTERS

Just about every character can be played by an actor of any gender.
Adjust pronouns accordingly.

PARENTAL OVERSIGHT

MOM

DAD

ALLIA

MAGDA

THE PRICE OF YOUTUBE FAME

TONI

DRAKE

JAMISON

MOM – offstage

TROLLZ

MAGGIE

KERRY

BOBO – a troll, either male or female

MONDO – a troll, probably male but could be female

VIRAL/RIVAL

AUSTIN

BRENT

AMELIA

BOSS

WORKERS

PINTEREST IS TOTALLY NOT MAKING YOU
ASHAMED OF YOUR LIFE

HUNTER

KYLI

MCQUAID

ROBINSON

FOLLOWERS

ASHLEY – Any gender, but same gender as Bailey. If male, Andrew.

BAILEY – Any gender, but same gender as Ashley. If male, Bart.

FOLLOWERS

THE LAST LIVING MYSPACE USER

TOM
KATHY
JANITOR
FIGURES

AUTHOR'S NOTES

1. Parental Oversight

2. The Price of YouTube Fame

3. Trollz

4. Viral/Rival

5. Pinterest is Totally Not Making You Ashamed of Your Life

6. Followers

7. The Last Living Myspace User

This play can be performed as a one-act or as a full-length play. For the one-act version, just perform four pieces in any order. For the full-length, include the next three.

PARENTAL OVERSIGHT

(A living room.)

*(**MOM** and **DAD** are looking at their phones.)*

MOM. Oh. Oh no.

DAD. Oh this is terrible.

MOM. I know. They're only getting worse.

> *(**ALLIA** enters, heading past.)*

DAD. Hold on there young lady.

ALLIA. I'm super busy so –

MOM. Not this time. You come here.

ALLIA. What?

MOM. We need to talk about this Instagram post.

ALLIA. That's private.

MOM. This is for your own good, sweetheart.

ALLIA. Can you just email your concerns to me?

DAD. No we cannot! Sit down, young lady.

MOM. As you know, your father and I are monitoring your posts on social media.

ALLIA. I know.

MOM. And then we find this.

> *(She takes out her phone.)*

Hold on I'm scrolling. "Breakfast today: Lucky Charms and OJ."

> *(**DAD** gets up and wanders about as if struck in the head.)*

DAD. What the heck is that?! No!!!

MOM. Charles. Please.

DAD. I can't even!

MOM. Honey, we said we were going to present a united front.

> (**MOM** *puts calming hands on* **DAD***'s shoulders.*)

DAD. Okay. You're right.

MOM. We still love her.

> (**DAD** *fights it.*)

Charles? We love our daughter. Right? We love our daughter.

DAD. I guess.

ALLIA. What's wrong with Lucky Charms and OJ?

DAD. Are you serious right now?! YOU DON'T KNOW WHAT'S WRONG WITH THAT?!

MOM. *(Holding him back.)* Whoah!

DAD. HOW DO YOU NOT KNOW?!

MOM. I think it's time for you to watch the video of the floof doggo again. Honey? Floof doggo.

> (*She puts her phone in* **DAD***'s face and calls up a floof dog video.*)

DAD. He's so beautiful.

ALLIA. What's all this about?

> (**MOM** *sits down with* **ALLIA** *while* **DAD** *looks at the video and wipes away tears.*)

MOM. Sweetheart, you took a picture of your breakfast and posted it on your Instagram.

ALLIA. Yeah?

MOM. And you can't see what's wrong with that.

ALLIA. No. It was what I had for breakfast.

MOM. How many likes did you get?

ALLIA. I just posted it this morning.

MOM. How many likes.

ALLIA. I don't know –

MOM. HOW MANY LIKES, ALLIA?!

> (*She shakes her phone in* **ALLIA***'s face.*)

NONE! ZERO. BECAUSE THAT WAS A BORING PHOTO.

ALLIA. IT WAS WHAT I ATE!

MOM. NO ONE CARES! I thought we raised you better than this. I thought you knew what would make a post on Instagram and what wouldn't. You know what I think – when I see a stupid photo of orange juice and cereal! I mean look at this. Look at the lighting on this, the angle, there's no composition, there's no sense of structure, it's A STUPID PHOTO OF BREAKFAST. When I see this I think – I have failed as a parent.

ALLIA. You haven't failed!

MOM. YOU TOOK A PHOTO OF JUICE YOU IGNORANT CHILD!

ALLIA. And cereal! There was cereal too!

MOM. NOBODY LIKED IT. Your own parents didn't even like it!

ALLIA. But that's you! You control that!

MOM. I'm not gonna like every stupid picture you put on Instagram! I have standards!

DAD. What your mother and I are trying to say is – you are terrible at Instagram.

ALLIA. That was one photo!

MOM. Oh honey – this is a symptom right here.

DAD. There was the photo of the sidewalk you posted. The photo of your shoes. You take a selfie every day of your outfit – like who cares? I don't care. I'm your father and I don't even care. You're not even wearing anything cute.

MOM. You have thirty-two followers, honey. That's not normal.

DAD. And half of them are probably Russian bots.

ALLIA. I don't judge myself by my followers!

DAD. But we do. And we have certain expectations in this family – and all of them involve you becoming internet famous.

MOM. You haven't even gone viral once. Why is that?

DAD. You know the Hendersons? Their daughter went viral with an inspirational tweet about Wonder Woman.

MOM. That tweet was amazing. It changed my life. I am a warrior now.

DAD. I know you are.

MOM. I don't need your validation anymore, Charles. And where are your inspirational tweets?

ALLIA. I'm focusing on Instagram!

DAD. Well I have looked at your Instagram and I am not inspired by you at all. One bit!

ALLIA. Instagram isn't supposed to be inspiring!

MOM. Did you just say that?!

DAD. THIS BREAKFAST PHOTO IS CRAP AND YOU NEED TO GET BETTER.

ALLIA. I'll do better I promise!

MOM. It's too late for that. Do you want to end up like your brother?

DAD. Let's not speak of him.

MOM. He only had nineteen followers.

DAD. No son of mine has only nineteen followers. He's dead to us. I unfollowed him.

MOM. So we have made a decision –

> (**MOM** *and* **DAD** *hold hands in solidarity.*)

And this wasn't easy for us –

DAD. Because I hate spending money on you –

MOM. Charles.

DAD. I mean I love you. And this means that we admit that we've failed –

MOM. We've hired an Instagram coach for you.

> (**MAGDA** *enters. She wears extreme makeup, maybe tall high heels – she looks striking.*)

This Is Magda. She's from somewhere in Eastern Europe so you know she's cool.

MAGDA. I am Magda. Look at me.

ALLIA. I don't even need an Instagram coach!

MAGDA. I have looked at all your photos. And I have liked...
NOTHING!

ALLIA. Mom –

MOM. This is for your own good, honey.

DAD. Listen to the nice lady.

MAGDA. I am not here to be babysitter. I am here to make
your Instagram amazing. Up. Get up.

ALLIA. I don't want to get up!

MAGDA. I SAID UP!

>   (**ALLIA** *jumps up.*)

Take out phone.

>   (**ALLIA** *takes out her phone.*)

Good. Yes.

MOM. I love that obedience.

MAGDA. QUIET!

MOM. Yes, ma'am.

MAGDA. I want you to take selfie for me.

>   (**ALLIA** *takes a selfie.*)

What is that.

ALLIA. A selfie?

MAGDA. What is face you made?

ALLIA. My selfie face?

MAGDA. Shut up. Do it again. Better face.

ALLIA. How do I make a better face?

MAGDA. BY MAKING BETTER FACE!

>   (**ALLIA** *takes a selfie with a different face.*)

NO.

ALLIA. You have a really difficult accent –

MAGDA. AGAIN.

>   (**ALLIA** *takes another selfie. She turns to look
>   at it.*)

MAGDA. You look at it again I slap phone out of your hand.

ALLIA. But how do I know if it's good if –

MAGDA. You feel it with heart not with eyes.

ALLIA. But –

MAGDA. Selfie again!

> (**ALLIA** *takes another selfie. As* **MAGDA** *shouts at her,* **ALLIA** *takes more selfies.*)

Selfie! Selfie! Selfie! Selfie! Selfie!

> (**ALLIA***'s exhausted.*)

Give me phone.

> (**MAGDA** *scrolls through the photos.*)

Crap. Crap. Crap. Crap. Crap…

> (*Short pause.*)

Crap. Your face is disappointing.

ALLIA. But I don't –

MAGDA. Watch.

> (**MAGDA** *takes a brilliant selfie.*)

ALLIA. Wow.

MAGDA. Yes. Wow yes.

DAD. I love that. I love what she just did. That was an inspiring face.

MOM. Shhh!

MAGDA. Now we post my photo.

> (*She posts it. Everyone waits.*)
>
> (*Bloop, a noise comes in.*)
>
> (**DAD** *and* **MOM** *burst with excitement and clap.*)

DAD. YESSS!

MOM. Someone liked it! Oh my gosh this is a dream come true!

ALLIA. It's her photo, Mom!

MOM. But honey, you're getting actual likes on your Instagram.

ALLIA. Of a selfie of her!

> *(Another bloop.)*

DAD. Wooooo!

> (**MOM** *and* **DAD** *high five.*)

MAGDA. You see?

ALLIA. That's ridiculous! Pictures of you get more likes than pictures of me!

> *(Another bloop.)*

DAD. Someone commented!

MOM. It's a miracle! We're great parents now!

ALLIA. No you're not!

MAGDA. Shhh! With your face maybe selfies are not for you.

ALLIA. What –

MAGDA. Shhhh. Quiet little bird. I want you to feel emotion.

ALLIA. Right now I'm feeling anger.

MAGDA. Good. Yes. Listen to it. Focus on hatred. What do you hate?

> *(Another bloop.)*

MOM. Ooooh.

DAD. Sweeet.

> (**ALLIA** *takes her phone – takes a photo of her parents.*)

MAGDA. Yes.

MOM. What are you doing?

MAGDA. If you light them from below they look more disgusting.

ALLIA. Ooh.

> (**ALLIA** *takes a photo from a lower angle.*)

DAD. Hey now.

MAGDA. Look at their old faces. So stupid old faces.

MOM. Would you stop that please?

> (**ALLIA** *takes more photos.*)

MAGDA. Good. Now post ugliest photo with funny caption.

> (**ALLIA** *posts the ugliest photo.*)

DAD. Honey. I want you to delete that photo.

> (*Bloop.*)

ALLIA. Ooh.

> (**MOM** *checks on her phone.*)

MOM. I look hideous!

> (*Another bloop.*)

People are making disparaging comments!

DAD. (*Looking at his phone.*) Someone posted a gif of a beached whale! Ah!

MOM. TAKE IT DOWN!

ALLIA. NEVER! I'M ONLY POSTING TERRIBLE PHOTOS OF YOU FROM NOW ON! I'M SURE THEY'LL GET LOTS OF LIKES SINCE THAT'S ALL YOU CARE ABOUT!

DAD. YOU WOULDN'T DARE!

ALLIA. WATCH ME!

> (*She runs off.*)

> (*After a moment:*)

MOM. I am loving her new edge.

DAD. It's about time she got a personality.

MOM. Really gonna help her get more followers.

DAD. Yeah.

MAGDA. It would also help if you got more disgusting.

DAD. On it.

> (*He starts making himself more disgusting as the lights go down.*)

THE PRICE OF YOUTUBE FAME

(Lights up on **TONI** *with an iPad.)*

MOM. *(Offstage.)* Toni are you doing your homework?

TONI. *(Yelling.)* I'm doing it!

MOM. *(Offstage.)* I know when you're lying!

TONI. I'm not lying I'm doing my homework leave me alone!

(Short pause.)

MOM. *(Offstage, yelling.)* I feel there's a fifty percent chance you're lying!

TONI. Stop yelling at me!

MOM. *(Offstage, yelling.)* I only yell because you lie!

TONI. All right let's see what my favorite YouTubers are up to today –

(Lights up on **DRAKE** *elsewhere onstage.)*

DRAKE. What up! This is Drake comin' at you from my new MAN-SHUN!

(He waves around at his mansion, which we can't see.)

Real Talk: Five point five million dollars. Your boy went on a SPENDING SPREE! Check out my MAN BUS!

(He points to his man bus.)

The best part is the hydraulics! YES! With me as always is my sweet sweet little brother Jamison, who is on loan from his school today.

*(***JAMISON*** *appears, looking ashamed.)*

JAMISON. Hey.

DRAKE. *(Rubbing* **JAMISON**'s *head.)* JAMISON! YES! AREN'T YOU SUPPOSED TO BE IN SCHOOL?!

JAMISON. Yes. You keep calling and saying that we have a family emergency.

DRAKE. BOOM! Big brother coming for ya! You are saved!

JAMISON. There was actually a discussion on *1984* that I wanted to participate in.

DRAKE. 1984 was lit!

JAMISON. Literature, yes. It's a book.

DRAKE. I mean the year. Reading is for suckers. I read something once, and I did not like it. And now look at me: WOOO! Let's take the tour of the new house!

JAMISON. Can I actually go home?

DRAKE. Check out this carpet, y'all! IT IS FUZZY. I love me some fuzzy carpet! It's like an animal came into my house like "oh this place looks nice" and then he DIED! And now we walk on him.

> *(He walks on the carpet and makes little noises like the animal is dying.)*

Ah! Ah! Ah!

JAMISON. So is there a family emergency?

DRAKE. There is. And it is related to this –

> *(He takes out a taser.)*

This is a police-grade taser, bro. POLICE GRADE.

JAMISON. I don't like this.

DRAKE. You're going to like it less when I tell you what it's for. But before I tell you what it's for I want to remind y'all out there to subscribe to my channel. Do it. DO IT NOW. OR YOU ARE DEAD TO ME.

JAMISON. I can't believe you get paid to do this.

DRAKE. I get paid so much, bro. That's why I can afford this 5.5 million dollar MAN-shun. WHAT! I am twenty-one years old, y'all. I make so much more money than your parents! BOOM!

JAMISON. I'm planning on going to college.

DRAKE. Bad idea, bro. College is where they put stuff INSIDE YOUR MIND. And it's so much better not to have that stuff. FIST BUMP. All right. Are you ready for the plan today?

JAMISON. Um...

DRAKE. But first I want to remind y'all out there that I have a new clothing line that is dropping this fall – you can get it online – and it is so lit – There's shorts and there are like shirts and YES. You can look just like me. IF YOU ARE MAN ENOUGH. Or woman enough. We don't have ladies' clothes yet but I make no judgments. Wear dudes' clothes if you want. You will probably feel better about yourself. If you have low self-esteem. Which is the worst, bro. I want to say something inspirational right now: This is from my heart.

(He taps on his heart.)

Believe in yourself.

JAMISON. That's it?

DRAKE. That is it. That is my message for the kids. Believe. In. Yoself. Or just give up. That works too. Deep moment OVERRRRR. Are you ready for the plan?

JAMISON. Not really, but I guess.

*(**DRAKE** puts his hand on **JAMISON**'s shoulder.)*

DRAKE. First thing we're gonna do: I'm gonna tase you.

*(**JAMISON** skitters away.)*

JAMISON. What?! No way!

DRAKE. Hear me out!

JAMISON. I'm not doing this!

DRAKE. What is wrong with you, bro?

JAMISON. What is wrong with you?

DRAKE. You won't even listen to my plan!

JAMISON. The first part involves you tasing me!

DRAKE. That's only the FIRST part! There's a SECOND part!

JAMISON. I don't want to hear it!

DRAKE. The second is: you get to tase me. And then we go back and forth.

JAMISON. Until when?!

DRAKE. Until one of us can't do it anymore. It's simple. Simplicity is genius. Gandhi said that.

JAMISON. Gandhi did not say that.

DRAKE. I am a Gandhi expert, bro. He also said, check out that booty.

JAMISON. He did not – that is not – that is not something Gandhi would say.

DRAKE. You don't know. He coulda said that. Just because it's not in your so-called "books" don't mean it's not truth. Gandhi also said that. Word.

JAMISON. There is so much wrong with you.

DRAKE. If that was true, why would I have a MAN-shun worth 5.5 million dollars? Huh? I own a helicopter. Do you own a helicopter? Do you? I can't hear you, bro.

JAMISON. I do not own a helicopter.

DRAKE. And I do. So that is why we're doing what I say. All right, ready? I'm gonna tase you first.

JAMISON. ...Fine.

DRAKE. You might want to take off your pants.

JAMISON. I'M NOT DOING THAT!

DRAKE. YOU HAVE ANGER ISSUES! Pants have metal in them – you never know what's going to happen.

JAMISON. Just do it already!

    (**DRAKE** *tases* **JAMISON.**)

AAAAAAAAAAAAAAAAH!

    (**JAMISON** *writhes in spastic pain and then collapses to the ground.*)

DRAKE. Duuuuude! Did you guys see that?! OMG, y'all!

    (**JAMISON** *is still twitching on the ground.*)

That's probably permanent brain damage right there. Whoah. This is beautiful. Jamison are you alive?

    (*He leans down.*)

I don't actually know how to check if he's alive or not but this is what they do on cop shows. Jamison. I am the voice of death. Are you alive?

JAMISON. ...Uhhh...

DRAKE. He's alive! For the record: you are a wuss. Sweet! So let's keep doing the tour of my house!

> (**DRAKE** *walks over* **JAMISON***'s body to a different part of the stage.*)

So they were telling me I had to have granite countertops and whatnot, and I was like, no man, I'm having granite cabinets. Check these out. Each of these weighs like four hundred pounds. You can't even open them. I hired like a mad scientist interior designer, it is ridiculous in here. Follow me!

> (*He moves to another part of the stage. He speaks directly out to the audience:*)

Are you jealous yet? Are you super jealous? I tricked out a bus, y'all.

TONI. Man.

DRAKE. I bet you wish you could be a YouTuber, huh?

TONI. Seriously.

DRAKE. Seriously.

TONI. What?

DRAKE. Loserssaywhat?

TONI. Are you talking to me? Through the internet?

DRAKE. How is it possible? Except through Skype or FaceTime or Google Hangout or many other apps?

TONI. But – I thought I was watching a video?

DRAKE. Toni, I know all about you.

TONI. You do?

DRAKE. Sure. I know about your time in Girl Scouts where you didn't sell a lot of cookies and nobody liked you, I know about that time you had a stuffed animal pig named Mr. Porkers – and you set him on fire –

TONI. That was an accident!

DRAKE. Was it? Was it, Toni?

TONI. ...No

DRAKE. And I know you want to be super famous.

TONI. How do you know all this stuff?

DRAKE. Oh I know many things. You see, I have achieved Nirvana. It happens once you get a million subscribers.

TONI. I didn't know!

DRAKE. Yeah – all your favorite YouTubers – Nirvana. All of them. We are like living gods now.

TONI. Whoah.

DRAKE. Yeah I know. Every time you watch one of our videos we get a small sliver of spiritual power, just like the ancient Greek gods. You can join us.

TONI. I want to. I want to be so famous. That's all I've ever wanted.

DRAKE. Yes. I know. Take my hand, bro. Join me in the Pantheon.

> *(He reaches out a hand to her.)*
>
> *(**TONI** gets up and stretches out to take it –)*
>
> *(Suddenly, they are in another place. Perhaps a cool sound effect happens.*)*

TONI. Am I...inside the internet?

> *(**DRAKE** looks around.)*

DRAKE. No this is Malibu.

TONI. How did I get here?

DRAKE. Because you believed in yourself. And I am now able to warp space and time to my will. Which is how I tased my little brother and he didn't get to tase me because I AM AWESOME, BRO. FIST BUMP.

> *(**TONI** tries to fist-bump him.)*

---

*A license to produce *Anti-Social* does not include a performance license for any third-party or copyrighted sound effects. Licensees should create their own.

COME ON.

TONI. Sorry!

(She fist-bumps him better.)

*(**DRAKE** takes out a contract.)*

DRAKE. Better. All right what I got here is a sweet offer of representation, brah. You join my enclave, you become part of my team, I cross-promote you on my channel – before you know it – you hit a million subscribers and you are golden.

TONI. What should I do on my channel?

DRAKE. What talents do you have? Can you do makeup? Can you sing?

TONI. No. I have no talent at all.

DRAKE. That's all good. I have no talent and look at me, brah. We'll figure it out. All right just sign here.

TONI. Should I read it first?

DRAKE. You're never supposed to read stuff before you sign it.

TONI. I'm gonna read it.

DRAKE. Your funeral.

(She looks it over.)

TONI. Why does it say I agree to give up my soul?

DRAKE. Wha-a-a-t?

TONI. Right here. It says I sign away my soul to you.

DRAKE. That's just standard legalese. I don't know what it means.

TONI. It means I give you my soul!

DRAKE. Psssht. I mean, if it that's important to you...

TONI. Wait a minute! You have no talent at all. You talk like a frat boy. You have power over time and space. You have six-pack abs even though I never see you working out! I know who you are!

DRAKE. Dude, brah. What.

TONI. It all makes sense now! I know how you got famous!

DRAKE. *(Voice of the devil.)* JOIN ME.

(*JAMISON leaps on* DRAKE*'s back and hits him with the taser.*)

JAMISON. Not today, Satan!*

DRAKE. AAAAAAAAAAAHHAAAAHAHHAH!

(DRAKE *collapses, twitching.*)

TONI. You stopped him.

JAMISON. For the moment. You need to run. That won't hold him for long.

TONI. Huh.

JAMISON. Come on, I'll help you escape!

TONI. Hey do you have a pen I could borrow?

JAMISON. Um...sure.

TONI. Thanks.

(TONI *signs the contract.*)

Hey can I see that taser?

JAMISON. Why –

(TONI *tases* JAMISON.)

AAAAAAAAAHHHHAHHHH! NOT AGAIN!

(JAMISON *collapses on the floor, twitching.*)

TONI. (*To the audience.*) So I'm super excited about my new channel. I mean, I could keep my soul, but imagine how much more fun my channel will be if I don't have a soul, right? It will be so much more entertaining for you! Remember to subscribe below – if you don't, I WILL FIND YOU.

(*Lights down.*)

---

*This line may be changed to "Not today!" or "Not today, evil one!"

TROLLZ

(A café.)

*(**MAGGIE** is sitting, looking around expectantly.)*

*(**KERRY** enters.)*

KERRY. Are you Maggie?

MAGGIE. Kerry? Oh my gosh it is so great to actually meet you in person! Should we hug?

KERRY. We should totally hug!

(They totally hug.)

I thought this day would never happen! I feel like I know everything about you already!

MAGGIE. I have to say, you are my absolute favorite Facebook friend.

KERRY. Oh.

MAGGIE. I love hearing about your nieces and your dog – oh my gosh your dog – she's so beautiful.

KERRY. My dog gives me faith in humanity. Maybe not humanity, maybe just dogs.

MAGGIE. That is so funny! You are so funny and your life seems so amazing!

KERRY. No your life is amazing! I love hearing about your Scentsy business! It's so great that you can sell so many products from the comfort of your own home!

MAGGIE. I know!

KERRY. And those selfies you take? When you're driving? So inspiring! I wish I looked like that when I was going seventy-five-miles-an-hour on the freeway.

MAGGIE. Can I tell you something? I cried when Facebook made that video of us celebrating five years of friendship online.

KERRY. Me too!

MAGGIE. Even though we weren't in any of the pictures together, it was so touching.

KERRY. I know. You know, your profile photo doesn't do you justice.

MAGGIE. Oh. That is so sweet.

>(**BOBO** *enters the café.*)

>(**BOBO** *has a bright pink wig, is possibly wearing clothes but could also be in a full-nude bodysuit.*)

Oh dang it.

>(**BOBO** *strolls around the café, perhaps putting its fingers on everything. Maybe scratching itself. Maybe getting uncomfortably close to people if there are others in the café.*)

KERRY. What?

MAGGIE. Don't look.

>(**KERRY** *looks.*)

I said don't look. It's a troll.

KERRY. Ah man.

MAGGIE. Just ignore him.

KERRY. How do you know it's a him? I can never tell with them.

MAGGIE. I don't really care about the gender of the troll, I just – shoot.

>(**BOBO** *sits at their table, right between them.*)

>(**BOBO** *doesn't say anything. Just stares at each of them in turn.*)

KERRY. This is actually a private conversation.

BOBO. This is a public space. If you didn't want to have a public conversation, then you shouldn't have met here.

MAGGIE. So um...anyway how is your new niece?

KERRY. Oh my gosh she is so adorable. She was seven pounds four ounces.

*(**KERRY** takes out his phone and shows a photo.)*

MAGGIE. She's beautiful.

BOBO. I mean, if you're into that sort of thing.

MAGGIE. What sort of thing?

BOBO. Come on. That's your baby?

KERRY. It's not my baby, it's my niece.

BOBO. Uh-huh. I mean...seven pounds four ounces? Kind of mediocre for a baby, right? I mean what percentile is that baby in? Like thirtieth? Her mom probably didn't eat enough.

KERRY. Her mom ate fine!

BOBO. And yet the baby was only seven pounds, so...and look I totally respect women, but just to play devil's advocate, what if she cared about her baby?

KERRY. Are you serious?

MAGGIE. Kerry? Just ignore the troll. Please. We're having a nice conversation. She's beautiful. You must be so proud.

BOBO. Yeah 'cause *you* worked really hard. I mean, thank goodness there's another human on the planet. We were running out.

*(**KERRY** ignores **BOBO**.)*

KERRY. So how's your Scentsy thing going?

BOBO. You know babies with low birth weight have lower IQs. There have been studies.

MAGGIE. It's going so great! The candles smell really wonderful and the essential oils will change your life.

*(**BOBO** scoffs.)*

KERRY. I love essential oils.

*(**BOBO** scoffs again. Louder.)*

MAGGIE. They can really help you relieve stress.

BOBO. OHHH-kay.

KERRY. Do you mind?

MAGGIE. Kerry –

BOBO. No go on and have your really scientific discussion about essential oils. I'm sure this is really grounded in fact.

KERRY. Essential oils are grounded in fact!

BOBO. *(Two thumbs up.)* Sure. Have you seen this article that I just googled?

KERRY. I'm not looking at that.

BOBO. You should look at my article. Check it out. It talks all about essential oils and how you're getting ripped off.

MAGGIE. Would you stop being such a troll?

      (**BOBO** *is offended.*)

BOBO. Oh I see how it is. I'm a troll, right? So I can't have an opinion on something? I'm just supposed to be totally silent over here? First of all, not all trolls are rude. Okay? I am one of the good ones. And second of all, we have something called the First Amendment in his country, which means I have the right to speak. And you can try to silence me all you want, but that makes you a fascist. How does that feel? Fascist.

KERRY. Why are you such a jerk?

BOBO. Nice. Resorting to personal insults.

MAGGIE. You called me a fascist!

BOBO. That is a statement of fact. Here are some qualities of fascists. Check out this article.

KERRY. Stop pushing articles at us! We don't want to read them!

BOBO. Oh I'm sorry did I offend you? Are you offended now? Do you need a safe space? Snowflake.

MAGGIE. We're trying to have a nice conversation, would you leave?

BOBO. WHAT AM I DOING? You know what Martin Luther King Jr. said?

KERRY. Don't quote Martin Luther King Jr.

BOBO. Oh I can't quote him? Because I'm a troll? Is that it? Only humans can quote him?

MAGGIE. Kerry – don't feed him. Just ignore him.

KERRY. Maybe we should go to another table.

BOBO. How do you think Martin Luther King Jr. would feel about only letting humans quote Martin Luther King Jr.?

MAGGIE. You know what? We're leaving.

BOBO. Running away from the truth.

> (**MONDO,** *another troll in a bright blue wig, enters from the other side of the room.*)

MONDO. Don't worry, I got this.

MAGGIE. We don't actually need your help.

MONDO. Essential oils…are essential. IT'S IN THE NAME.

BOBO. *(Standing up.)* Essential to WHAT?!

MONDO. To LIFE. How do you not get that?!

BOBO. Oh sure right you can put oil on yourself and change your brainwaves! That sounds totally logical!

> (**MONDO** *and* **BOBO** *are standing over* **MAGGIE** *and* **KERRY,** *arguing.*)

MONDO. Check out this article from Fox News.

BOBO. You did NOT just give me something from Fox News!

MONDO. They do SERIOUS reporting!

BOBO. They are a propaganda arm!

MONDO. Oh and the other news organizations aren't?! Here's a list of lies in the mainstream media!

BOBO. That is a biased list of lies! The list itself is lies! Here's a video of all the lies from Fox News!

MONDO. THE VIDEO WAS DOCTORED!

> (**MAGGIE** *and* **KERRY** *get up to leave.*)

MAGGIE. We're just gonna see ourselves out.

KERRY. It was really nice meeting you.

> (**MONDO** *comes over to them.*)

MONDO. I just wanted to say that not all trolls are like this.

MAGGIE. Okay.

MONDO. So don't judge all of us based on the actions of one troll.

KERRY. I wasn't.

MONDO. That's totally racist, by the way. Doing that. I think you guys are the real racists.

MAGGIE. I'm not, actually. I'm not.

BOBO. *(Coming over to intercept them.)* Everybody's racist. There have been studies.

MONDO. What does that even mean?! How can everybody be racist?!

BOBO. It's called implicit bias!

> (**MAGGIE** *grabs* **KERRY** *and pulls him to another spot on the stage.*)

MAGGIE. So um anyway...it was really great meeting you.

KERRY. I'm sorry about the trolls.

MONDO. *(Following.)* Or you're *sorry* about the trolls? What's that supposed to mean?

MAGGIE. Ignore them.

KERRY. Before we go, I wanted to show you a new picture of my dog.

MAGGIE. I really want to see her.

> (**KERRY** *looks over at the trolls and hands his phone to* **MAGGIE.***)*

She's so pretty!

> (**MONDO** *is looking over her shoulder.*)

MONDO. Why is she pretty? Because she's female? If this was a male dog, would you use that language?

MAGGIE. I just thought she was objectively pretty.

MONDO. Mm-hmm. But not handsome. Or a good boy. You see what you're doing there?

MAGGIE. Sorry.

MONDO. I just wanted to say I'm super feminist. The biggest feminist, actually. Like, if feminists had a king and I believed in monarchies, I would totally be king of the feminists.

KERRY. Nice to know.

MONDO. What's that supposed to mean?

KERRY. It doesn't mean anything!

MONDO. So you're just going to dismiss me, is that it? You don't feel like you have to back up any of your opinions? You're here in a public space and you can't handle defending your beliefs? Ohhh-kay. I guess that's how you like it, then.

KERRY. I can defend my beliefs just fine, thank you.

MONDO. You haven't even shared a single article.

KERRY. About what?!

MONDO. Wake up, Sheeple! Don't you see what's going on here? You're believing what they want you to believe!

BOBO. (*Coming over.*) Literally, LOLing right now. Sheeple? You're the sheeple!

KERRY. I am not a Sheeple! First of all, there have been plenty of studies showing that you only believe what you want to believe.

> (**BOBO** *and* **MONDO** *get on opposite sides of* **KERRY.** **MAGGIE** *moves away.*)

MAGGIE. Kerry don't talk to them!

BOBO. Those studies are biased!

KERRY. Not according to PolitiFact!

MONDO. Oh please?! PolitiFact is biased! Didn't you see the tweets from one of their employees?!

KERRY. What do the tweets of one employee have to do with the organization?!

BOBO. Did you just say that?! You don't think those employees are putting their fingers on the scale?!

KERRY. That's what you'd like to believe, isn't it? That there's no objective fact! That's the stupidest thing I've ever heard!

MONDO. Oh and now you're back with the personal insults!

BOBO. What it looks like to have no argument!

MAGGIE. Kerry! Get out of there! You're arguing with trolls about nothing!

BOBO. I was four years in the military so I know all about this!

KERRY. Who cares if you were in the military?!

BOBO. I know that I can fight you!

MONDO. That'll solve everything won't it!

KERRY. If you're threatening to fight someone on the internet you've already lost!

BOBO. Because you're afraid to fight me!

MAGGIE. KERRY NO! GET AWAY FROM THEM!

> (**KERRY** *is trapped. The* **TROLLS** *surround him, getting closer and closer and louder and louder.*)

KERRY. BOTH OF YOU ARE IDIOTS!

MONDO. IF YOU LOOKED AT THIS ARTICLE YOU'D KNOW THAT WASN'T TRUE!

BOBO. OPEN YOUR EYES!

KERRY. ARRRRRRRRRRGH!!!!

> (**KERRY** *collapses onto the ground.*)

MAGGIE. Kerry?

> (*Slowly,* **KERRY** *gets back up. He now has a troll wig on his head. If possible, he is wearing a nude bodysuit under his clothes and can slowly be taking off the clothes during this sequence, but it is not required.*)

No... Kerry? What's going on? What happened to your hair?

> (**BOBO** *and* **MONDO** *watch him.*)

KERRY. Not all trolls are bad...

MAGGIE. No! NOOO!

KERRY. Maggie...

MAGGIE. Fight it! You're not one of them!

KERRY. *(Trying to fight.)* I...can't...stop arguing...about nothing on the internet...

MAGGIE. Come back to me, Kerry! You can do it!

KERRY. I have this overwhelming urge to present myself as an expert on health care.

MAGGIE. But you don't know anything about health care!

KERRY. I know, but on the internet I'm an expert! And I feel the need to add LOL after everything!

MAGGIE. Stop!

> *(**MAGGIE** runs up to him and grabs him.)*

Let's share photos! Let's talk about babies like we used to!

KERRY. It is too late for me...must...share...video of Alex Jones.[*]

MAGGIE. Not him! Anyone but him!

> *(**MONDO** and **BOBO** each put a hand on **KERRY**'s shoulder.)*

BOBO. It's time.

MONDO. Join us.

KERRY. Where are we going?

BOBO. Reddit. It's glorious there.

MONDO. You'll fit right in.

BOBO. Say goodbye to your old life.

MAGGIE. Nooooo!

> *(**BOBO** and **MONDO** drag **KERRY** offstage.)*

Damn you Facebook!

> *(She shakes her fist at the sky.)*

I'm never using you again!

> *(She slides her phone away from her.)*

Never! You're awful! I'm never looking at you again!

---

*"Alex Jones" can be changed to "*Talking Points Memo.*"

(She tries not to look at her phone.)

MAGGIE. I'm completely done with you!

(She's moving closer to her phone.)

I wouldn't even look at my phone except I have my step-counter on there and there's no point in moving if it's not being recorded in my step-counter. And I have like a lot of pictures so it's cool.

(She picks up her phone.)

But I am turning off my notifications and...

(She looks at Facebook.)

Like. Like. Like.

(She breaks down crying as the lights fade on her.)

Like. That was cute. Like. Like... Sad emoji... Like...

VIRAL/RIVAL

(A terrible office of soul-destroying cubicles.)

*(**AUSTIN** has been here forever. His soul is mostly destroyed.)*

*(**BOSS** comes in and claps for everyone's attention.)*

BOSS. All right let's hit those targets. These terrible insurance policies aren't going to sell themselves.

AUSTIN. *(On the phone.)* Yes, hello, this is Austin with Consolidated Insurance –

(They've hung up.)

(He dials again.)

Yes, hello this is Austin with –

(They've hung up again.)

(He dials again.)

Yes, hello this is Austin with Consolidated Insurance. We have a special offer for – yes, ma'am. Sorry I didn't understand I was calling during dinner. Yes I – no my family is not proud of me. That's right, I am ashamed of my existence, yes, thank you for pointing out that I am a cancerous boil on the rear end of humanity. That really helps me see things clearly. While I have you on the phone –

(They've hung up.)

*(**BOSS** comes over.)*

BOSS. New guy can I have a word with you?

AUSTIN. It's Austin and I've been here four years.

BOSS. Whatever. Do you like your job?

AUSTIN. Sure. Yes. There's nothing I like more than facing constant rejection and pain. Luckily, I have a lot of antidepressants that I'm taking and I have four therapists so it helps –

BOSS. I didn't ask for a movie. If you want to keep your job, do better. Okay? Happy smiles on the phone. Or you are out on the street.

AUSTIN. Of course.

BOSS. Oh and I'm lowering your pay just for fun. Come on people let's see if we can take money from the elderly!

(**BOSS** *claps and moves on.*)

(**AUSTIN** *is about to dial again when* **AMELIA** *enters. Maybe music plays.* Maybe a light shines on her. Maybe she's just really pretty.*)

AUSTIN. (*A little too happy.*) Amelia!

AMELIA. Oh hi Austin.

(*Pause.* **AUSTIN** *stares at her in wonder.*)

AUSTIN. Hi.

AMELIA. How are you doing today?

AUSTIN. Much better, thanks.

AMELIA. What?

AUSTIN. Nothing! Um...are you doing anything this weekend?

AMELIA. Probably just watching Netflix and petting my cat. Like I do every weekend. Alone. Single. Available. Kind of wistfully looking off into the distance and imagining my life with someone special. What about you?

AUSTIN. Same. I mean... I don't know. Um... Maybe...if you're not busy...and you were free...and maybe...

(**BRENT** *enters.*)

---

*A license to produce *Anti-Social* does not include a performance license for any third-party or copyrighted music. Licensees should create an original composition or use music in the public domain. For further information, please see Music Use Note on page 3.

(**BRENT** *is cool.*)

BRENT. What's up office workers? Sorry I'm late. They had two-for-one wings at Hooters. Where I am friends with all the waitresses.

AMELIA. *(Not impressed.)* Wow.

BRENT. Yeah. Definitely wow. How's it going, Amelia?

AMELIA. Oh you know.

BRENT. Looking foxy today. Me likey.

AUSTIN. We were actually in the middle of a conversation, Brent.

BRENT. Were you? Was it awesome? Were you pouring your heart out? Is there a Loserville convention nearby that you were thinking of attending?

AUSTIN. That's not really a thing.

BRENT. Let me tell you something, Austin: Here at Consolidated Insurance, I run the show. Got it? You are on the bottom and you are always going to be on the bottom. Hey Amelia –

AMELIA. I'm going to the bathroom.

BRENT. Enjoy.

> (**AMELIA** *leaves.*)
>
> (**BRENT** *moves over to his cubicle, puts his feet up.*)

Yessir, life is good.

BOSS. All right people! COME ON. Let's sell that insurance!

AUSTIN. Man, working here is like eating ice cream all day except the ice cream is made out of failure and sadness.

BRENT. What's that you just said?

AUSTIN. I said, working here is like eating ice cream all day except the ice cream is made out of failure and sadness.

BRENT. That's pretty funny.

> (**BRENT** *takes out his phone and conspicuously tweets that.*)
>
> (**AUSTIN** *watches him. Then takes out his phone.*)

AUSTIN. Excuse me, did you just tweet what I said?

BRENT. What about it?

AUSTIN. I mean, I said that. That was my saying.

BRENT. Yeah, and I tweeted it.

AUSTIN. But your tweet doesn't say anything about me.

BRENT. Should it?

AUSTIN. It should say, according to my co-worker Austin, and then you could tag me –

BRENT. Why would I tag you?

AUSTIN. Because I said it. I created that idea.

BRENT. Yeah and I tweeted it.

AUSTIN. But you wouldn't have been able to tweet it unless I said it.

BRENT. *(Mocking him.)* Oh gee. Sorry. You should've thought of that first. Check it out, four people have already liked it.

AUSTIN. I haven't had four people like a tweet of mine in months!

BRENT. Welp. There you go.

> (**AMELIA** *returns. She checks her phone.*)

AMELIA. Oh man how true. I'm gonna retweet this.

> (*She retweets it.*)

Brent? Is this your tweet?

BRENT. Yup.

AMELIA. This is exactly how I feel. It's like this tweet is a window into my soul; it's everything I've always wanted to say but couldn't find the 280 characters for. I mean I thought you were just a jerk but now that I see this tweet, I know…you're pretty special.

BRENT. Thank you.

AUSTIN. What?!

BRENT. Austin's jealous. He wishes he came up with the tweet.

AUSTIN. I did come up with the tweet and you stole it!

AMELIA. Oh Austin. That's sad. The lies.

BRENT. I know. He should get help.

AMELIA. I look at you and I think of a homeless kitten. If only you had the help you needed. I'll pray for you.

(*She goes back to her seat.*)

AUSTIN. (*Hissing.*) I said that and you stole it!

BRENT. How can I steal it?! It's words! It's in the air! You don't own the air! That's insane!

AUSTIN. It was my idea!

BRENT. Did you copyright it? Didja? Did you send money to the government? Did you say, before I speak I want you to know that all ideas contained in my words belong to me and me alone? No, you did not say that! Therefore, that saying was public domain!

AUSTIN. Fine, here's an idea that belongs to me and me alone, I hate you and I will destroy you!

(**BOSS** *returns with phone.*)

BOSS. Brent, did you write this tweet? On company time?

BRENT. Austin claims it was his tweet. He likes to lie.

BOSS. Well, Austin. Did you spend your very valuable insurance-selling time creating this tweet?

AUSTIN. Um...

BOSS. And may I remind you that I like firing people for no reason.

AUSTIN. Brent was the one who tweeted it.

BOSS. Are you sure about that?

AUSTIN. ...Yes.

BOSS. Because this is one heckuva tweet.

(**AUSTIN** *sits back down.*)

BRENT. Thank you.

BOSS. So clever. The wit. What are you doing here on the selling floor? Your creativity belongs in management. This tweet...

(*She looks at her phone and shakes her head in wonder.*)

BOSS. I've rarely seen a tweet so beautiful. And it's already got a hundred likes.

AUSTIN. A hundred likes?!

BOSS. So many retweets.

BRENT. *(Chuckling.)* R.I.P. my mentions! Am I right?

> *(He high fives the* **BOSS**.*)*

Holy cow Dustin Diamond just retweeted it!

> *(***BRENT** *raises his arms in victory.)*

> *(Word is beginning to spread.)*

AUSTIN. Who's Dustin Diamond?

BOSS. Screech, from *Saved by the Bell*. Come on, catch up.

BRENT. *(Looking at his phone like it's about to explode.)* What is happening?!

BOSS. You're going viral!

> *(***AMELIA** *gets up.)*

AMELIA. What's going on?!

BOSS. BRENT'S GOING VIRAL! EVERYONE BRENT'S GOING VIRAL! THIS IS A CODE RED! THIS IS A CODE RED!

BRENT. WOOOOOOOOOOOOO!!!!!!!!

> *(Other* **WORKERS** *drop what they're doing and rush over to check out* **BRENT***'s phone.)*

> *(***AUSTIN** *tries to ignore them.)*

WORKER 1. George Takei liked it!

WORKER 2. *(Overlapping.)* Zach Galifianakis just retweeted it!

WORKER 3. *(Overlapping.)* Kelly Clarkson liked it!

> *(***AUSTIN** *puts his head down and picks up the phone.)*

AUSTIN. *(On the phone.)* Yes hi this is Austin at –

BOSS. LEBRON JAMES LIKED IT!

> *(Everyone stops.)*

AMELIA. WHAT?! LEBRON JAMES!

BRENT. HE'S FOLLOWING ME ON TWITTER NOW! LEBRON JAMES IS FOLLOWING ME ON TWITTER!!!! – HE JUST SENT ME A DM!

(*Everyone jumps up and down and cheers.*)

BOSS. Read it!

BRENT. Dear Brent: Awesome Tweet. Here are two courtside tickets for my next game. XOXO LBJ, aka the King.

(**BRENT** *holds his phone in front of him, shaking.*)

BOSS. What does X O X O mean?

AMELIA. Hugs and Kisses!

BOSS. LeBron James is giving you hugs and kisses?

BRENT. He's very affectionate.

AMELIA. This is so amazing!

ALL. WOOOOO!

AUSTIN. (*On the phone.*) Yes, hi this is Austin at Consolidated Insurance and –

BRENT. THIS IS THE GREATEST DAY OF MY LIFE! ALL OTHER DAYS OF MY LIFE PALE IN COMPARISON TO THIS RIGHT HERE! I AM SO GLAD I TWEETED THAT!

AMELIA. Marry me! Marry me now!

BRENT. I THINK I CAN DO BETTER!

AMELIA. YOU PROBABLY CAN!

BRENT. STEVEN SPIELBERG IS CALLING! EVERYONE SHUT UP!

(*Everyone is quiet and huddles around* **BRENT**.)

Yes hello Mr. Spielberg.

Yes it was a brilliant tweet, wasn't it? It wasn't quite *E.T.* but it was close.

(*He holds the phone to his chest.*)

BOSS. (*Thumbs up.*) Good one!

(**BRENT** *listens to the phone again.*)

BRENT. Well I'm exploring my options with the tweet right now. Whether to go with a TV series or a film, uh-huh... uh-huh... Chris Evans is gonna play me? I'll get back to you – Hey Steve – Steve – I don't even get out of bed for less than two million, so... All right done.

(*He hangs up.*)

AAAAAAAAAAAAAAAAAHHHHHH!

(*The other* **WORKERS** *start celebrating.*)

BOSS. TODAY IS CANCELLED! BRENT IS OUR GOD!

AUSTIN. Yes, hi this is Austin at –

(**AUSTIN** *stares at the celebration in dumbstruck horror.*)

WORKERS. (*Chanting.*) BRENT BRENT BRENT BRENT!

(**BRENT** *waves his hands for silence.*)

BRENT. I just wanted to say that it was great working here, and even though I am now so much more famous than all of you, and I'm going to have an amazing, wonderful life now, I still think that you guys are tops.

WORKERS. WOOOO!

BRENT. I never learned any of your names because I didn't care about any of you. But you can still say...you knew me. LET'S GO TO HOOTERS! SOME OF THE WINGS ARE ON ME!

(*Everyone cheers and chants and stomps offstage.*)

(*Pause.*)

(**AUSTIN** *picks up the phone.*)

AUSTIN. Hi this is Austin from...Consolidated Insurance... and...maybe you could brighten my day by buying a policy – no? Eat rocks and die? Okay, thanks.

(*He dials another number as* **AMELIA** *comes back in.*)

Hi this is – hold on – something more important just happened. You want insurance? Really? I don't care.

(He hangs up.)

AMELIA. I was halfway there and then I realized we were going to Hooters, which I hate and –

AUSTIN. That Hooters is surprisingly close.

AMELIA. Yeah.

AUSTIN. Hey look um…I realized something today. Life is short and you have to go after what you want.

AMELIA. Yeah?

AUSTIN. And uh…you know how you're staying home with your cat this weekend? Maybe um…maybe you could stay home with your cat and me and my cat. I'll bring him over. He's almost friendly.

AMELIA. You wanna do that?

AUSTIN. Because my heart feels full when I look at you.

*(**AMELIA** puts her hand to her heart and crosses over to him.)*

AMELIA. That's the sweetest thing anyone's ever said to me.

AUSTIN. Really?

AMELIA. Yeah. That was so beautiful.

AUSTIN. Thank you. I mean it.

(They are very close. About to kiss.)

AMELIA. Hold on one second.

(She takes out her phone and tweets something.)

AUSTIN. Did you just tweet that?!

(Lights down.)

PINTEREST IS TOTALLY NOT MAKING YOU ASHAMED OF YOUR LIFE

(A living room. Maybe a couch. Maybe a kitchen table upstage with a highchair next to it.)

*(**KYLI** is blowing up balloons. A laptop sits on the couch next to her, closed. **HUNTER** enters upstage with a shopping bag.)*

HUNTER. How many plates do you think we're gonna need?

KYLI. Don't tell me you got plates already.

HUNTER. Yeah I stopped off at Party City.

KYLI. You went to Party City?!

HUNTER. It was on the way home.

KYLI. Hunter, we don't even have a theme for the birthday party yet.

HUNTER. So?

KYLI. So how are we gonna get plates when we don't even have a theme?! That's crazy.

HUNTER. I figured these would be okay.

KYLI. What did you get?

*(**HUNTER** reveals the plates. They are blue.)*

HUNTER. Um...I got blue ones.

KYLI. This is not happening.

HUNTER. What's wrong with blue plates?!

KYLI. What if they don't fit our theme?

HUNTER. We'll just make the theme "blue."

KYLI. What is wrong with you?

HUNTER. I'm sure blue will be acceptable.

KYLI. Acceptable? That's your goal for Milo's first birthday party? Acceptable. That's what you're striving for? You think the other moms and dads are going to come to this birthday party and be like, "Wow this is so *acceptable*! What an *acceptable* party! I'm totally going to share photos online of how *acceptable* this party is! Weeee!"

HUNTER. Maybe you're overthinking this birthday party?

KYLI. I'm sorry, you're right. I'm going a little overboard. I just need some good ideas from Pinterest and then I'll be fine.

>   (**KYLI** *opens her laptop.*)

HUNTER. Don't go on Pinterest. Please. Don't do it.

KYLI. It has so many great ideas for crafts, Hunter.

HUNTER. Every time you go on that site you change!

KYLI. That's absurd.

HUNTER. It's true! You start taking unnecessary pauses all the time! Like you're just thinking – and you're not saying what's on your mind! It's like you're becoming British.

KYLI. How am I supposed to get ideas for the birthday party without going on Pinterest?

HUNTER. Maybe we don't even need to have a theme! We just have cake –

KYLI. Just cake?! Just blue and cake! That's your idea! You're honestly suggesting WE DON'T HAVE A THEME. What do we do for gift bags then? Just paper sacks?! Here you go, here's a paper sack filled with our failed dreams from our pathetic themeless party!

HUNTER. What if we didn't have gift bags?

>   (**KYLI** *looks at him with contempt.*)

KYLI. Who are you?

HUNTER. Do we need gift bags for a birthday party? When we were growing up we didn't have gift bags and we lived.

KYLI. I'm gonna pretend you didn't say that.

HUNTER. Kyli –

> (**KYLI** *looks at her laptop and raises her hand for silence.*)
>
> (*Pinterest loads. Soft, somewhat menacing piano music plays.* [Whenever **KYLI** is looking at Pinterest, the music plays. When she stops looking at Pinterest, the music stops.])
>
> (**KYLI**'s *demeanor changes completely as she looks at the site.*)

KYLI. This is cute.

HUNTER. What is?

> (*Pause.*)

What is – what is cute?

> (*Pause.*)

Did you see something cute?

KYLI. Very cute.

HUNTER. What?

> (*Pause.*)

Please just tell me and don't pause like that. It worries me.

KYLI. Why should it worry you? That I take pauses?

HUNTER. Because I don't know what's going on in your head during the pauses.

> (*Pause. She looks at him.*)

You just look at me. And you don't say anything.

KYLI. I'm evaluating.

HUNTER. What? What are you evaluating?

KYLI. Are you afraid of what I'm evaluating?

HUNTER. No I just want to communicate with you.

---

*A license to produce *Anti-Social* does not include a performance license for any third-party or copyrighted music. Licensees should create an original composition or use music in the public domain. For further information, please see Music Use Note on page 3.

KYLI. I see.

(*She turns back to the computer.*)

What about a theme of – zoo animals – for the birthday party.

HUNTER. That sounds good.

(*Pause.* **KYLI** *looks at* **HUNTER**.)

What?

KYLI. It sounds good?

HUNTER. Yes.

KYLI. Zoo animals sounds good. For a theme?

HUNTER. Yeah I think it's fine. We could put animals around and…you know like an elephant and maybe some tigers and lions.

(*Pause.*)

KYLI. Lions and tigers – at a zoo.

HUNTER. We could make cartoon animals – paint smiles… on them…

(*Pause.*)

KYLI. You want to paint smiles on them.

HUNTER. Yes?

(*Menacing pause.* **KYLI** *approaches* **HUNTER** *very deliberately.*)

What? Is there something I'm missing? Why are you taking all these menacing pauses?!

(*Menacing pause.*)

KYLI. Why do you think they're menacing? Are you hiding something?

HUNTER. No!

KYLI. You seem like you're hiding something.

HUNTER. I'm not! I just don't know what's going on in your head and it's scaring me! What do you want from me?! I THINK ZOO ANIMALS ARE FINE!

KYLI. (*Exploding.*) ZOO ANIMALS ARE NOT FINE!

HUNTER. Why did you suggest them then?!

KYLI. I WAS TESTING YOU! And you have failed!

HUNTER. What is wrong with zoo animals?!

(Pause.)

KYLI. That's your question?

HUNTER. Pinterest does this to you! Every time you get on Pinterest you get like this!

KYLI. You think a party celebrating the prison-industrial complex and the enslavement of animals is a proper theme for a birthday party? You want to "decorate" with a parade of effigies of sacred creatures – with cartoon smiles – erasing their suffering, erasing their reality, and you think this is the proper way to memorialize one entire year of life of our only child.

HUNTER. So you're saying zoo animals are out?

(Pause.)

So what other ideas do you have then?

KYLI. I'm interested in your ideas.

HUNTER. I don't have ideas! I want to know your ideas!

(Pause.)

KYLI. So it's my role to come up with the theme.

HUNTER. All right, tell you what, let's do Barney.

(Pause.)

Let's not do Barney. How about Mickey Mouse?

(Pause.)

Transformers?

(Menacing pause.)

Where is this music coming from? Is this the music on Pinterest? It's driving me insane.

(He spots the laptop, rushes over to it, and closes it.)

(Music stops.)

There.

(**KYLI** *changes back to normal.*)

KYLI. Wow it's like my mind just cleared.

HUNTER. There's something about that website that is not cool.

KYLI. You're right – I've been spending too much time on the internet, let's come up with a fun idea for a party together. Okay?

HUNTER. Okay!

KYLI. Hug?

HUNTER. Oh my gosh yes!

(*They hug.*)

KYLI. I don't mean to be mean to you but there's just so much pressure to make this party amazing.

HUNTER. Yeah, I know. When Gemma and Andre had that Gilded Age-themed party for little Bartholomew?

KYLI. With the ice sculptures?

HUNTER. And those gift bags with the handwritten notes saying how much they appreciated our luminosity?

KYLI. I literally died when I got those. Luminosity?!

HUNTER. Who says that?

KYLI. I had to look that word up.

HUNTER. I hated them for that party. They made all other birthday parties look like trash fires in comparison. Except for Scott and Scott's party for Janelle.

KYLI. That's two dads, that doesn't even count. We can't compete with them.

HUNTER. I just don't want to feel terrible afterwards.

KYLI. That's why we've got to have a great party! We need to beat them! We just need a killer idea.

HUNTER. You're right!

KYLI. Think!

HUNTER. And you think.

(*They think.*)

(*They've got nothing.*)

(They think again.)

(They've got less than nothing.)

KYLI. Let me just check Pinterest –

HUNTER. No!

KYLI. I won't even be on it for long.

HUNTER. You know what it does to you.

KYLI. I promise. I've got it under control. Just for a minute. I just need a theme and then I'm done.

> *(**KYLI** goes over to the laptop. Opens it.)*
>
> *(The music returns.)*
>
> *(**KYLI** changes.)*

HUNTER. See anything good?

> *(Venomous pause.)*

Kyli? Have you um...seen anything?

> *(Pause.)*

KYLI. Have I seen anything?

HUNTER. Theme-wise?

KYLI. You want to know if I've seen anything theme-wise.

HUNTER. Right.

> *(Pause.)*

KYLI. For the birthday party.

HUNTER. Yes!

KYLI. How do you feel about clowns?

> *(Pause.)*

HUNTER. How do you want me to feel about clowns?

> *(Pause.)*

KYLI. It's just a question.

HUNTER. Like a circus? Like a circus theme?

> *(Pause.)*

Um...if that's what you want, then that's what I want.

KYLI. I see.

(Sad pause.)

HUNTER. But I also love clowns. I think.

KYLI. You love clowns.

HUNTER. Yes?

KYLI. You've never told me you loved clowns before.

HUNTER. I didn't know until just this moment.

KYLI. What else haven't you been telling me?

HUNTER. I'm telling you everything!

KYLI. And yet you never mentioned these clowns. That's disappointing.

(There's a knock at the door.)

HUNTER. *(Nervous.)* Are we expecting someone?

KYLI. Two gentlemen.

HUNTER. What gentlemen?

KYLI. To help with the birthday party.

HUNTER. But we don't even know what the theme is!

KYLI. But they are here. Answer the door, Hunter.

HUNTER. ...Okay.

*(**HUNTER** answers the door.)*

*(**MCQUAID** and **ROBINSON** enter. They are quietly menacing. Perhaps they speak like British thugs.)*

MCQUAID. Hello there.

ROBINSON. Greetings.

HUNTER. Hi. Um...I'm not sure what Kyli has hired you to do.

MCQUAID. He's not sure.

ROBINSON. He doesn't know.

MCQUAID. That's funny.

(Pause.)

Ha ha.

(Pause.)

HUNTER. What exactly are you here for?

ROBINSON. The birthday party.

HUNTER. Are you clowns?

> *(Menacing pause.)*

MCQUAID. Clowns.

ROBINSON. You said clowns.

MCQUAID. You think we're clowns?

HUNTER. Ha ha ha.

> *(He rushes over to **KYLI**.)*

What are these people doing here?

> *(Pause.)*

KYLI. What did they say they were here for?

> *(**MCQUAID** cracks his knuckles loudly.)*
>
> *(**ROBINSON** looks like he's getting ready for a fight.)*

MCQUAID. We'll just make ourselves at home then.

KYLI. They're probably just here to help with the birthday party.

ROBINSON. That's right.

KYLI. Maybe you could help inflate the balloons.

MCQUAID. Oh we'll help inflate – the balloons – all right.

ROBINSON. Yeah we loooove inflating...balloons.

> *(They both stare at **HUNTER** and take a balloon.)*
>
> *(They inflate the balloons very slowly, staring menacingly at **HUNTER**.)*
>
> *(**HUNTER** goes over to **KYLI**, unnerved.)*

HUNTER. Are you sure they're here to help?

KYLI. Why wouldn't they be here to help?

HUNTER. They seem –

> *(**MCQUAID** lets all the air out of his balloon, staring at **HUNTER** the entire time.)*

HUNTER. They're like goons. Why did you bring goons into our living room?

KYLI. They're here to help with the party.

HUNTER. How?

KYLI. Well that depends on you, doesn't it?

> (**ROBINSON** *lets the air out of his balloon.*)

HUNTER. What do you mean?

> (*Pause.*)

KYLI. You never told me about your love for clowns. And now you love clowns. I find that a little too convenient.

HUNTER. Is this about the party?

KYLI. Of course this is about the party. Why wouldn't this be about the party?

HUNTER. I don't like this anymore.

KYLI. (*Showing him the computer.*) Look at these cake pops – little clown heads. Do you like them?

> (**ROBINSON** *and* **MCQUAID** *gather menacingly, still half-inflating balloons and dropping them on the ground.*)

HUNTER. …I don't know…

KYLI. What about these hat decorations.

HUNTER. I don't know.

KYLI. Don't you like them?

HUNTER. I'm not sure.

KYLI. People on Pinterest like them.

HUNTER. I don't need to look on Pinterest! I feel good about my life.

> (*Pause.*)

KYLI. Should you?

HUNTER. Yes! Please! I'm sorry if I did anything wrong! Let's just turn off Pinterest and lead a normal life!

KYLI. You'd like that, wouldn't you? That would be easy. McQuaid. Robinson. I think it's time to start the party.

MCQUAID. Absolutely.

ROBINSON. I've been waiting for this.

> (**HUNTER** *lunges and shuts the laptop.*)
>
> (*Music stops.*)
>
> (*Everyone snaps out of it.*)
>
> (**MCQUAID** *and* **ROBINSON** *sound very different – not like British thugs anymore.*)

KYLI. Oh my gosh I feel so much better.

MCQUAID. Why am I in a stranger's house?

ROBINSON. We're so sorry. Sometimes he just wanders away from me! I am so sorry! Come on pookie.

MCQUAID. I love your drapes, by the way.

ROBINSON. They don't care!

> (**ROBINSON** *escorts* **MCQUAID** *out.*)

KYLI. I'm so sorry. Sometimes I get a little stressed from Pinterest and I start acting weird.

HUNTER. I get a little stressed out when you're on Pinterest!

KYLI. I don't know what it does to me.

HUNTER. Everything on that website just shows you how much better everyone is than you! You can't just have a store-bought cake, you have to farm your own wheat and then hand-grind it into flour with your own artisanal wood tools purchased from Amish craftsmen. And your cartoon hippos better be perfect, dang it, or you are the worst failure in human history! And your child is going to grow up hating you for your immense suckitude! Don't you see? Pinterest is making you like this! You're judging everything because you're judging it against obsessive people who ONLY MAKE CAKES. And they post photos of AMAZING CAKES to show you just how pathetic your cakes are! WELL I LIKE PATHETIC CAKES! THAT'S WHY I MARRIED YOU!

KYLI. What?

HUNTER. 'Cause you're not perfect, but you're good enough.

KYLI. You married me because I was good enough? Like "this one's okay, I guess I'll spend the rest of my life with her."

HUNTER. Okay, that came out wrong. Let's have an okay birthday party for Milo. No theme. No gift bags. A crappy cake.

KYLI. What about his friends?

HUNTER. He has no friends he's one!

KYLI. I don't know.

HUNTER. That's the beauty of this age. He won't remember anything. Nothing we do now matters at all.

KYLI. I'm not so sure about that.

HUNTER. I'm just saying that this birthday party is totally pointless and stupid.

KYLI. My mom's coming for it.

HUNTER. But I don't like her, so I don't care. Kyli: Let's be mediocre parents.

KYLI. I like the sound of that.

HUNTER. It's so much less work!

KYLI. I know!

HUNTER. We can read those books we've always wanted to read.

KYLI. I don't know if I even remember how to read.

HUNTER. We can binge-watch TV shows.

KYLI. I've heard *Game of Thrones* is nice.

HUNTER. Very nice. Whaddya say? Let's not invite anyone to this stupid birthday party and totally half-ass it.*

KYLI. Done!

> *(Short pause.)*

Should we have a theme?

HUNTER. Blue.

> *(They hug.)*
> *(Lights down.)*

---

*The end of this line can be cut.

FOLLOWERS

(A high school gym.)

*(**BAILEY**, dressed in a basketball uniform, is stretching.)*

*(**ASHLEY**, also dressed in a basketball uniform, enters and starts stretching next to **BAILEY**.)*

ASHLEY. Crazy weekend, huh?

BAILEY. What?

ASHLEY. You must've had a crazy weekend.

BAILEY. It was fine.

ASHLEY. Huh that's funny.

BAILEY. Why?

ASHLEY. I just figured you were like abducted or something.

BAILEY. Um...no.

ASHLEY. That's weird, 'cause I noticed you didn't like any of my tweets this weekend. What's up with that? And I couldn't really think of any other explanation for why you wouldn't like my tweets.

BAILEY. Um...

ASHLEY. I figured you were probably kidnapped and had to jump out of a speeding car or something, and you were probably lying injured in a ditch, bleeding out – I mean that's the only logical reason you would like exactly ZERO of my tweets this weekend.

BAILEY. I guess maybe I didn't see them.

ASHLEY. Or maybe it was just too much effort for you to like my tweets, right? Like you're looking at your phone, and you could tap the heart, but that's SOOO hard to do sometimes, right? Like, SOOO much effort for that.

BAILEY. Probably you're just not showing up in my feed.

ASHLEY. Can I check?

BAILEY. What?

ASHLEY. Give me your phone, I'll check your feed. I want to see.

BAILEY. My battery's really low right now, so.

ASHLEY. Really? 'Cause I saw that you liked Chelsea's tweet from this weekend. I guess you really liked it. 'Cause you retweeted it. Which is weird, because it seems like, from my perspective, her tweet was mediocre at best. And yet you retweeted it. I mean, that's crazy, right? Why would you retweet something that was mediocre and yet at the same time never retweet any of my really funny, really awesome tweets?

BAILEY. Maybe your tweets just aren't as good as you think they are.

ASHLEY. Excuse me?

BAILEY. I mean I have standards. For a retweet. Like a tweet has to meet a certain threshold, because I don't want to just be retweeting everything, you know? Nobody likes that person.

(**ASHLEY** *regards* **BAILEY** *with a stare of death.*)

ASHLEY. You know who else nobody likes? The person who never retweets anything. Because that person is dead weight. You're like a drag on my followers. Because my followers see that nobody else is liking my tweets, so they don't like it, because they don't want it to get weird.

BAILEY. That's kind of messed up.

ASHLEY. I've liked tweets of yours that aren't even that good.

BAILEY. Whatever.

ASHLEY. I've retweeted tweets of yours that were desperate attention grabs. Out of pity. I retweeted out of pity!

BAILEY. Sure you did. That's why you have a lot less followers than me.

ASHLEY. You did NOT just go there.

BAILEY. I wasn't gonna say it, but it's true.

ASHLEY. The only reason I have less followers than you is because you don't retweet my tweets! If you retweeted them, people would see how amazing I am, and they would follow me! I'm totally unfollowing you. That's it. We are done. I am unfollowing.

BAILEY. Okay.

(*Pause.* **BAILEY** *keeps stretching.*)

ASHLEY. You'd just let me go, wouldn't you? You wouldn't even care. You'd just go on with your life!

BAILEY. WHAT DO YOU WANT FROM ME?

ASHLEY. I want you to say you're sorry!

BAILEY. Fine! I'm sorry!

ASHLEY. Are you?

BAILEY. Arrrgh!

ASHLEY. I want you to tweet an apology to me!

BAILEY. I didn't do anything wrong!

ASHLEY. Seriously. You ignored my tweets.

BAILEY. Maybe your tweets deserved to be ignored.

(**BAILEY** *moves elsewhere to stretch.*)

(**ASHLEY** *whips out her phone.*)

ASHLEY. 4:27 p.m. I think pandas are basically doggos with hands.

(*Pause.*)

THAT WAS AN AWESOME TWEET.

BAILEY. Are you for real? That tweet sucks! It makes no sense.

ASHLEY. I added a gif of a panda! LOOK AT IT!

BAILEY. You can't just get a like for a stupid gif!

ASHLEY. I WAS CLEVER YOU INSECT.

BAILEY. Pandas aren't like doggos at all! Pandas are like furry burglars!

(**FOLLOWER 1** *runs in and is right behind* **BAILEY**.)

FOLLOWER 1. *(Forming a heart with her hands.)* Like!

> *(Pause.* **ASHLEY** *stares at* **FOLLOWER 1.***)*

ASHLEY. Um...what the heck is that?

BAILEY. What?

ASHLEY. The person right behind you.

BAILEY. One of my followers. They keep changing their names so I never know who anybody is.

FOLLOWER 1. *(Forming a heart with her hands.)* Like!

ASHLEY. Your followers follow you in real life?

BAILEY. Yours don't?

ASHLEY. No.

BAILEY. My followers are super dedicated.

FOLLOWER 1. *(Heart.)* Like!

BAILEY. It can get a little annoying.

FOLLOWER 1. Laughing emoji!

ASHLEY. Will she like things I say?

> *(Moves a little toward her.)*

Pandas are just doggos with hands?

> *(No reaction from* **FOLLOWER 1.***)*

BAILEY. Sorry.

ASHLEY. Maybe if you repeat it then she can follow me?

BAILEY. I don't know, my followers have high standards too.

FOLLOWER 1. *(Heart.)* Like!

ASHLEY. Okay fine, what about this tweet? This one is great.

> *(Reads off her phone.)*

Adaxafil says its side effects include loss of limbs. What's in these pills? Chainsaws?

> *(***ASHLEY** *stares at* **BAILEY.** *No reaction.)*

OH COME ON.

BAILEY. WHAT?!

ASHLEY. THAT'S AN AMAZING TWEET!

BAILEY. I hate it when people try too hard with their tweets.

FOLLOWER 1. *(Heart.)* Like!

> (**FOLLOWER 2** *runs in, gets right behind* **BAILEY.**)

FOLLOWER 2. *(Heart.)* Like! RETWEET!* I hate it when people try too hard with their tweets.

> (**FOLLOWER 3** *runs in, gets right behind* **FOLLOWER 2.**)

FOLLOWER 3. *(Heart.)* Like!

> (**BAILEY** *starts doing lunges across the stage, all of her* **FOLLOWERS** *right behind her.*)

ASHLEY. Seriously? You got three likes for that?! And I didn't get any for my pandas tweet??!

BAILEY. Why are you obsessed with pandas? Let it go!

ASHLEY. IT WAS FUNNY.

BAILEY. NO ONE ELSE THOUGHT SO.

ASHLEY. Share your followers with me.

BAILEY. No.

ASHLEY. Please. I need them. Explain to them how great I am.

BAILEY. My followers respect truth.

> (**BAILEY** *starts lunging in the opposite direction – the* **FOLLOWERS** *follow very closely.*)

FOLLOWER 1. *(Heart.)* Like!

FOLLOWER 2. *(Heart.)* Like!

FOLLOWER 3. *(Heart.)* Like!

ASHLEY. Please! I'm begging you! Let them know how funny I am! Tweet: you should follow Ashley. She's amazing. I'll even write it for you! Give me your phone!

BAILEY. Sorry.

ASHLEY. Can you stop doing that for a second and give me your stupid phone?!

BAILEY. Gotta get ready for the game.

---

*"Retweet!" should be yelled in a throaty, disconcerting way, almost like a frog yelling "ribbit."

FOLLOWER 1. Like! RETWEET! Gotta get ready for the game!

FOLLOWER 2. *(Overlapping, not in unison.)* RETWEET! Gotta get ready for the game!

FOLLOWER 3. *(Overlapping.)* Like!

> *(**FOLLOWERS 4, 5,** and **6** run in and get behind the other **FOLLOWERS**.)*

FOLLOWERS 4, 5 & 6. *(Overlapping.)* Like!

ASHLEY. Oh come on that was just a stupid cliché sports thing!

BAILEY. It was inspirational.

ASHLEY. It was a cliché! It wasn't funny! It wasn't clever! It was just dumb!

BAILEY. And yet...so many likes.

ASHLEY. I can say inspirational sports stuff too! We're taking it one game at a time!

> *(Nothing happens.)*

I'm just trying to stay within the system! Can't think too much about...stuff...

> *(**ASHLEY** breaks down.)*

I feel so alone.

> *(Waits.)*

NOBODY EVEN LIKES THAT?!

> *(**BAILEY** puts a hand on **ASHLEY**'s shoulder.)*

BAILEY. No.

> *(**ASHLEY** sniffles.)*

Hey. You just have to believe in yourself.

> *(The **FOLLOWERS** Go Crazy.)*

FOLLOWERS. *(At different times, overlapping, very rapidly.)* Like! RETWEET! You just have to believe in yourself! So true. It me. Mood.

> *(If you have more actors, more and more **FOLLOWERS** enter, retweeting and liking.)*

ASHLEY. Arrrrrrrrghghghghg.

BAILEY. You know there is one way you can get more followers.

ASHLEY. Sell my soul?

BAILEY. No. You can retweet my tweet.

ASHLEY. Never.

BAILEY. Have it your way. But my tweet is just waiting for you.

>*(Staredown.)*

ASHLEY. I'm not doing it.

BAILEY. Good. Don't do it.

ASHLEY. I'm not going to.

BAILEY. I'm sure you're not.

ASHLEY. Definitely not.

>*(Pause.)*

Because that would be pathetic.

BAILEY. Yep. Sure would.

ASHLEY. Yes it would.

>*(Pause.)*
>
>(**ASHLEY** *falters.)*
>
>*(She thinks about it. Cracks.)*
>
>*(She speaks like it's a death sentence.)*

Re...tweet. You just have...to believe in your...self.

>*(She hangs her head.)*
>
>*(Waits.)*
>
>*(Nothing.)*

BAILEY. Maybe nobody likes you.

FOLLOWERS. Like! RETWEET! Maybe nobody likes you.

>*(Lights down on the noise of retweeting and liking.)*

THE LAST LIVING MYSPACE USER

(A post-apocalyptic nightmare.)

(Wind howling.)

(Arctic noises.)

(Maybe some trash blowing through.)

(Lights up very dimly on **TOM**. *He wears ragged clothing, as if he's survived a nuclear holocaust.)*

(Elsewhere onstage we see other **FIGURES**, *standing completely still with their arms at their sides, as if they are frozen in time.)*

TOM. *(Calling out.)* Hello? Is there anybody out there? Anyone?

(Wind howling.)

That's okay! It's fine. I'm still having fun. On MySpace. Anyone else on MySpace? Anyone?

(A tumbleweed blows through.)

Whee.

(Pause.)

That's okay I'm just gonna update my page like I do all the time. Let's get some music going.

(A song like "My Humps" plays.*)

---

*A license to produce *Anti-Social* does not include a performance license for "My Humps." The publisher and author suggest that the licensee contact ASCAP or BMI to ascertain the music publisher and contact such music publisher to license or acquire permission for performance of the song. If a license or permission is unattainable for "My Humps," the licensee may not use the song in *Anti-Social* but should create an original composition in a similar style or use a similar song in the public domain. For further information, please see Music Use Note on page 3.

TOM. Yes. This is my jam.

> (*He sings along pathetically for a moment.*)
>
> (*He is alone, trying to sing a pop song into the howling void.*)
>
> (*He stops.*)

Anybody? Does anybody...want to be on my friend list? My top ten friends? The number-one spot is pretty much open.

> (**TOM** *shivers.*)

This place used to be so amazing. All my friends were here. Britney Spears was here. And now... Britney?! BRITNEY ARE YOU OUT THERE?

> (*He waits for an answer. Nothing.*)
>
> (*A* **JANITOR** *enters, mopping.*)

Hey! Hey you there!

JANITOR. Just doin' my job, man.

TOM. Are you signing up for MySpace? You should totally sign up for MySpace!

JANITOR. I'm just paid to clean up, sir.

TOM. But you could be my friend. I could friend you. You could be my number-one friend. We could listen to music together. You could come to my page; we could listen to music! Do you like Nickelback? 50 Cent? I've got some great Black Eyed Peas.

JANITOR. Look, I don't make friends at my job.

> (*The* **JANITOR** *approaches one of the* **FIGURES.**)

TOM. What are you doing?

JANITOR. These accounts are dead. Haven't logged in in years. I'm deleting them.

> (*He tips over the* **FIGURE** *and starts dragging it offstage.*)

TOM. What?! But they could come back!

JANITOR. I don't make the rules, buddy.

*(The **JANITOR** drags the **FIGURE** all the way offstage. Returns a moment later, goes to another one.)*

TOM. No no no these are my friends!

JANITOR. Tom, your friends aren't coming. They don't care about MySpace. They've moved on.

TOM. Where did they go?

JANITOR. How should I know? Facebook? Instagram? Twitter? Maybe they quit social media altogether and are living rewarding, healthy lives in the real world.

TOM. What?!

JANITOR. It happens.

TOM. That's horrible!

JANITOR. If you want my advice: get out now. Before we shut this whole thing down.

TOM. But what's going to happen to my music choices?

JANITOR. Nobody cares about your music choices. All right? Suck it up.

*(The **JANITOR** goes up to another **FIGURE**.)*

(Drags it offstage.)

TOM. You're a murderer!

JANITOR. Just doin' my job. I got about a billion of these to clean up. Welp.

*(The **JANITOR** goes up to **KATHY**.)*

*(**KATHY** startles awake.)*

KATHY. Hello?

TOM. Hello!

JANITOR. All right time to go –

(He's about to delete her.)

TOM. No no no she's moving! Look! She's logged in!

KATHY. Where am I?

TOM. This is MySpace! It's so wonderful! You're back!

KATHY. *(Confused, looking around.)* My web browser must have auto-completed me here.

TOM. I know! And it's great!

JANITOR. All right kids. It's my break time. I'm gonna go surf for a while. I'll be back.

(*The* **JANITOR** *shuffles off.*)

KATHY. You're Tom? How do I know you?

TOM. I think I met you in a corporate retreat in 2003.

KATHY. Huh.

TOM. Kathy, right? And then we friended each other on MySpace.

KATHY. I haven't used this account in like a decade.

TOM. No one has!

(**KATHY** *looks around.*)

(*Howling wind.*)

KATHY. What happened to this place?

TOM. It's great! It's really great!

KATHY. There's no one here.

TOM. ...Yeah. I mean that's part of its charm, I think. As far as dystopian nightmare landscapes filled with nothingness go. It's the quiet. You want to listen to some Black Eyed Peas?

KATHY. Are they still alive?

TOM. They're always alive on MySpace.

(**TOM** *starts the sad-sounding version of the pop song again.**)

KATHY. This song is pretty terrible.

TOM. Yeah.

(*The song stops.*)

---

*A license to produce *Anti-Social* does not include a performance license for "My Humps." The publisher and author suggest that the licensee contact ASCAP or BMI to ascertain the music publisher and contact such music publisher to license or acquire permission for performance of the song. If a license or permission is unattainable for "My Humps," the licensee may not use the song in *Anti-Social* but should create an original composition in a similar style or use a similar song in the public domain. For further information, please see Music Use Note on page 3.

So what do you want to do? We could message each other. We could just hang out. We could make a list of things we like or don't like. There's so so much to do here.

KATHY. Um...

TOM. We could get to know each other. I made a list of books I like, and music I like, and my favorite movies, and then you could make your lists, and then we could...share them.

KATHY. Right. I think I'm just gonna go.

TOM. No! Stay. Please. I think I'm falling in love with you.

KATHY. I barely know you! I think I met you once!

TOM. And yet here we are, and you can look at my profile and learn everything about me! And I can look at your profile – you like *Gilmore Girls*, and *American Beauty*, and the music of Christina Aguilera. WE'RE PERFECT FOR EACH OTHER!

KATHY. But that's like superficial crap that I liked fifteen years ago! I've changed my mind about *American Beauty*. I still like *Gilmore Girls*.

TOM. But that's who we are inside, isn't it? A list of superficial crap? That's our deepest self.

KATHY. No! Tom. I left MySpace because there were so many creepers here. And seedy ads for generic Viagra.

TOM. And now the creepers have left and nobody advertises here anymore. It's perfect! I can be your creeper. And you can be my seedy knockoff Viagra ad.

KATHY. I have a life in the real world.

TOM. This is better than the real world!

KATHY. Is it?

TOM. Yes! Don't you feel it? Look at me.

(She looks at him.)

What if you were looking for someone your whole life, and the only reason you didn't find that person was that there were so many other terrible people in the way?

KATHY. I have dated a lot of terrible guys.

TOM. Right? And here we are. Together! We're connected. Remember when you were in grade school and it was like, "Would you go out with me if I was the last guy on Earth?" Well here we are! We're the last people on MySpace. And we can love each other. Just think about it! All this –

> (*Wind howling.*)
>
> (*A tumbleweed blows through again.*)
>
> (*Perhaps something falls over.*)

All this is ours now. We have all of MySpace to ourselves.

KATHY. I was thinking about deleting my Facebook account because of all the political fighting.

TOM. Right! There's no politics here. There's just...dumb stuff. Don't you miss the world from 2003? When everything was simpler?

> (**KATHY** *thinks about it.*)

KATHY. I don't know, Tom. I don't know that I can walk away from the modern world, even if it is a mess. I mean I have Netflix now. It's pretty amazing. And a smartphone. I have the internet in my hand all the time! I am always connected to everything. And that's... destroying me.

> (*She takes a moment.*)

I can't ever stop to think because it's like people are shouting at me all the time. And everything is a disaster and there's so many things to be fighting for, but all the fighting just seems to be online and nothing ever changes. And even though I always have all this incredible stuff at my fingertips, what do I do with it? I'm either angry, or anxious, or stressed out, or watching a really adorable video about dogs and cows being friends, and then I'm anxious and stressed out that I watched that video because there was so much to be angry about that I was missing.

I don't know. Maybe it's better here with you. Maybe we do have a connection. Maybe we can love each other. Maybe I should stay here in MySpace.

(A moment.)

TOM. Let's share our top ten movies.

(With each movie they get closer together.)

KATHY. Number Ten: *Steel Magnolias*.

TOM. Number Ten: *Apocalypse Now*.

KATHY. Number Nine: *When Harry Met Sally*.

TOM. Number Nine: *American Pie*.

(They are touching now.)

KATHY. Number Eight –

(She stops.)

(She resumes the blank position.)

(Pause.)

TOM. What's Number Eight?

(No response.)

(Wind howling.)

Kathy?

(No response.)

This isn't funny. Are you still there?

(He waves his hand in front of her face.)

Are you still logged in?!

(Desperate.)

My Number Eight is *Dumb and Dumber*. I like stupid movies sometimes. Do you like stupid movies?

(No response.)

...Kathy?

*(The **JANITOR** enters.)*

JANITOR. Welp.

*(He approaches **KATHY**.)*

TOM. No no no she just logged out for a second she'll be right back!

JANITOR. They never come back, buddy.

TOM. No please! Delete a different account! I don't even know her last name!

JANITOR. Sorry, pal. Gotta remove the dead accounts.

> *(The **JANITOR** goes up to **KATHY**.)*
>
> *(Drags her offstage.)*
>
> *(**TOM** watches.)*
>
> *(**TOM** stands there, alone. Turns away.)*
>
> *(**KATHY** comes back in behind him.)*

KATHY. Number Eight is *Dumb and Dumber*.

> *(**TOM** runs up and hugs her.)*

Sorry I was just loading the app on my phone. I had to log out for a second.

> *(She looks at him.)*

You're crying. I didn't know you could cry in MySpace.

TOM. I guess you can.

> *(They hold on to each other as the lights fade.)*

KATHY. Number Seven...*Finding Nemo*.

TOM. Number Seven...

> *(Lights fade out completely.)*

End of Play